CW00543223

Flies for Selective Trout

FLIES FOR SELECTIVE TROUT

COMPLETE STEP-BY-STEP INSTRUCTIONS ON HOW TO TIE THE NEWEST SWISHER FLIES

DOUG AND SHARON SWISHER

Skyhorse Publishing

Skyhorse Publishing books may be purchased in bulk at special discounts for sales promotion, corporate gifts, fund-raising, or educational purposes. Special editions can also be created to specifications. For details, contact the Special Sales Department, Skyhorse Publishing, 307 West 36th Street, 11th Floor, New York, NY 10018 or info@skyhorsepublishing.com.

Visit our website at www.skyhorsepublishing.com.

10 9 8 7 6 5 4 3 2 1

Library of Congress Cataloging-in-Publication Data is available on file.

Cover design by Tom Lau
Cover photo credit by Doug and Sharon Swisher

Print ISBN: 978-1-5107-1716-9
Ebook ISBN: 978-1-5107-1717-6

Printed in China

Contents

ACKNOWLEDGMENTS

Family for support and encouragement.

Doug Brewer for his help creating "action dubbing" and other materials through the years.

Tony and Kathi Tomsu for their friendship and support.

Nick Lyons for his suggestions and referrals.

Dynamite day on the kick boat.

INTRODUCTION

Great rod holder when releasing.

Fifty years ago, during the period when Carl Richards and I were working on the development of the no-hackle dry fly, emergent dun imitations were tied mostly with lots of bushy hackle. As the transition was made toward more natural, realistic-looking flies, we had to search for new tying materials, especially to imitate the freshly hatched species. Our first attempt at this project resulted in the use of a clump of deer hair. Our immediate success ratio skyrocketed, and this type of pattern was very easy to tie. Our next improvement was fanning the wings and splitting the tails to form outriggers and was also easy to do. But we felt the need for something else! The clump of deer hair seemed a bit heavy and *clubby* for the wings, so we replaced it with a matched pair of duck quill wings. This ended up being the final step in making a really polished-looking No-Hackle Dun.

We had all the right ingredients; the only problem was mounting the wings properly. If they were attached so that they radiated from the sides of the body, they provided super floatation. If they were cut wide and short, they were extremely durable. The greatest no-hackle flytier I ever knew was Bill Monaghan, from Detroit. We often fished together on Michigan's famed Au Sable River. I could easily catch over twenty trout on his No-Hackle Duns. He and Carl Richards were the best flytiers I ever knew. They were both dentists; maybe their ability to tie such great flies was due to the fine work they constantly performed with their hands. The three of us often fished together, and of course it normally ended up being a contest of who caught the most fish on a single fly. Bill usually won, but Carl and I had our moments.

Back in the 1980s, right after *Selective Trout* was first published, many fly-tying books came on the market that were pushing the merits of the types of flies Carl Richards and I developed, like the No-Hackle Dun, Hen Spinner, Emerger, and Still-Born. Those were types of flies that had never been written about before. Then, a few years later, in the early 2000s, the emphasis switched drastically to what I would call streamer and attractor patterns. This book covers a few of the no-hackle types and many of our new attractor flies, like glow-in-the-dark, ultraviolet, brush flies, advanced pupas, and our action-dubbing versions. Also included are tips on how to fish them and where they were developed. Most of this change came about because of all of the new materials and tying techniques now available, making our new flies even more exciting.

A Montana beauty!

Parachute Madam X.

DRY FLIES

In this section of the book, we'll first cover three of the most famous no-hackle flies, the No-Hackle Dun, the Duck Quill Emerger, and the Hen Spinner. Then, we will show you how to tie some of the more important flies we developed since the no-hackle era. These include the Madam X, which is the first dry fly with rubber legs; the Parachute Madam X, which is well known all over the world; the Button Fly, the first hatch simulator utilizing a rubber post; and the Double Parachute Hopper, which has a parachute hackle at each end, and the rear one under the wing has a rubber post. There are several more dry flies that have given us many wonderful days fishing on rivers and lakes.

No-Hackle Pale Morning Dun

Duck Quill Emerger

Hen Spinner

Floating Nymph

Hi Float Emerger

Madam X

Parachute Madam X

Button Fly

Double Parachute Hopper

Speckl-X

Para-Tractor

Hare & Herl

Dancing Caddis

Clumpa

Tiger Tail

Yummy, yucky, but delicious.

No-Hackle Pale Morning Dun

It seems evident that many of the best flytiers are dentists. At least that was the case with my dental friends, Carl Richards and Bill Monaghan, who were from Michigan and who both tied great flies, especially no-hackles. The key on making a durable no-hackle was having a pair of duck quill wings that look like naturals and mounted so that they radiate from the sides of the body and, even more importantly, are slightly wider than the naturals. As a flytier, it is relatively easy to mount long, skinny wings, but extremely difficult to position short, wide wings on a tiny dun. That is where extreme fly-tying skill is required, in some cases taking many years of practice. Hundreds of perfectly matched quills usually must be selected to gain this skill level.

The other important factor is quill selection. Only the highest quality quills will stand up to the rigors of dozens of feeding fish. The application of synthetics and various varnishes simply does not do the job. Also, attaching the wings at exactly the right spot on the body is critical. They should be mounted at the bottom edge of the body. In that manner, they act as a second set of outriggers, along with the split tails, to maintain both balance and floatation.

Besides blue-winged olives, the pale morning dun is one of the super mayfly dun hatches of the world. I have fished the pale morning dun all over the United States and in other countries like England, New Zealand, Canada, Australia, South Africa, and Russia. The Au Sable River in Michigan has an exceptional hatch of these little pale-bodied duns and is where I first encountered them back in the 1950s. Sometimes we fish them on a dead drift, and other times the fish like the movement of skittering them.

NO-HACKLE PALE MORNING DUN MATERIALS

Hook standard dry fly hook

Thread 8/0

Tail gray hackle fibers

Body yellow dry fly dubbing

Wing matched pair of duck quill feathers

NO-HACKLE PALE MORNING DUN TYING INSTRUCTIONS

Step 1. Tie in split tails of good quality hackle fibers. Making a little ball of dubbing above the barb makes it easier to split the tails and keep them in place.

Step 2. Dub to a point three eye-lengths from eye of hook. Dub a little bump at the point where the wings will go, as it helps the wings spread.

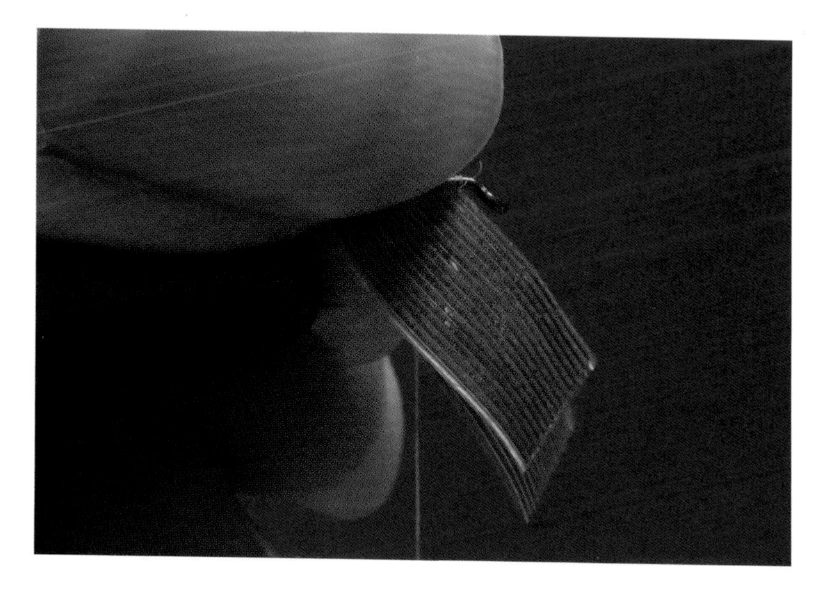

Step 3. Tie on a fairly upright wing, holding both pieces of quill in one hand while making two loose wraps of thread around the quills and hook, then tighten slowly. Make a few more wraps, then secure with a half hitch.

Step 4. Cut off excess quill and tie down the butts. Secure with a half hitch.

Step 5. Dub over wing tie in and to the eye of the hook. Tie off fly and glue.

Duck Quill Emerger

This emerging pattern has gulled more rising trout into its degree of realism than any other fly in my box. This is especially true on the spring creeks of Montana and the super clear waters of New Zealand. The good news is that it is not hard to tie. When you are dealing with the construction of a pair of fully developed upright mayfly wings, it usually takcs years of practice to learn how to mount them, that is, after you have acquired the ability to select the perfect quill. For the Emerger, you do not have to be so picky about your hand-eye coordination. Wings can be shorter and skinnier, making them much less difficult to position and attach to the body. If needed, great Emergers can usually be fashioned by trimming the wings off an old, beat-up no-hackle with a pair of scissors.

DUCK QUILL EMERGER MATERIALS

Hook standard dry fly hook

Thread 8/0

Tail gray hackle fibers

Body dark olive dry fly dubbing

Wing matched pair of duck quill feathers

DUCK QUILL EMERGER TYING INSTRUCTIONS

Step 1. Tie in split hackle fibers. Make a little ball of dubbing above the barb; it makes it easier to split the tails, as well as helps hold them in place. Secure with a half hitch. Dub to a point three eye-lengths from the eye of hook.

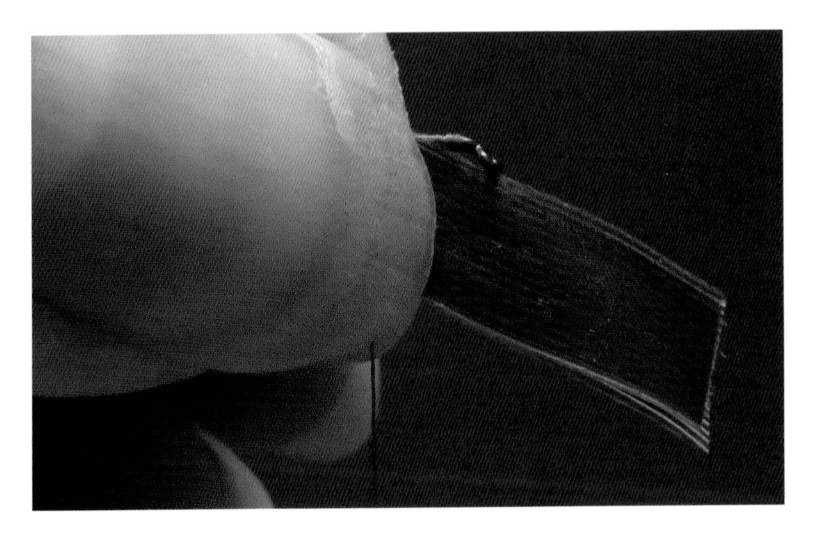

Step 2. Tie on a short wing, holding both pieces of quill in one hand while making two loose wraps of thread around the quills and hook and tightening slowly. Make a few more wraps of thread and secure with a half hitch.

Step 3. Cut off excess quill and tie down the butts. Secure with a half hitch.

Step 4. Dub over tie in and to the eye of the hook. Tie off fly and glue.

Don't breathe—the Tricos will get ya!

Hen Spinner

The Hen Spinner is the most versatile hatch matcher we developed during our study for *Selective Trout*. It was originally designed to match the hatch during spinner falls, but we have since discovered if proper hen tips are selected, it works great as a freshly hatched dun or as an Emerger. At times, it is deadly as a wet fly. Just think about it—the spinners are in the process of dying as they drown in the current, without the ability to climb out of the stream. The next time you encounter a spinner death fall, fish it wet and you might be surprised. Let your fly go to the end of the drift before recasting. Some tie concave up and others concave down. Take your pick, the trout do not seem to care.

HEN SPINNER MATERIALS

Hook standard dry fly hook

Thread 8/0

Tail tan hackle fibers

Body reddish-brown dry fly dubbing

Wing hen hackle tips

HEN SPINNER TYING INSTRUCTIONS

Step 1. Tie in split tails, making a little ball of dubbing above the barb makes it easier to split the tails. Secure with half hitch. Dub to a point three eye-lengths from the eye of the hook. This is where the wing will go.

Step 2. Tie in wing. Take a broad hen hackle tip and cut some of the fibers off the stem, do not strip them off. Tie in the broad hen hackle tip, concave side down,

crisscross the thread to hold the wing in place, letting the stem of the hackle hang out to the other side. Secure with half hitch.

Step 3. Bend the butt of the stem back along the shank and tie it down with a few wraps. Secure with half hitch. Tie in the other wing the same way.

Step 4. Dub around the wings and to the eye. Tie off and glue.

Alternate method. Underside—many people tie the fly with the wing concave up.

Floating Nymph

Small nymphs, like pale morning duns and blue-winged olives, are extremely difficult to see in the currents, but when you observe wings of the hatching duns on the water, you know they are present. Before this discovery, back in the early 1970s, nymphs were designed to be fished subsurface, usually near the bottom. After observing this phenomenon of nymphs riding on the surface, which occurred mainly on the Livingston, Montana, spring creeks, we started tying nymphal patterns that floated just like a dry fly. They were extremely difficult to see, but very deadly. To improve visibility, we started dying our tippets, and eventually the whole leader and line system, chartreuse.

This floating nymph has a ball of dubbing on the wing case area of the fly that can be made as large as one wants to make it. It is the most time-consuming part of tying the fly. If the ball is too small, the fly will not float well. Using good dry fly dubbing is very important, as well as adding some floatant. We fish it a lot on Poindexter Slough by Dillon, Montana.

FLOATING NYMPH MATERIALS

Hook standard dry fly hook

Thread 8/0

Tail brown hackle fibers

Abdomen dry fly dubbing

Wing Case dry fly dubbing

FLOATING NYMPH TYING INSTRUCTIONS

Step 1. Tie in tail of good quality hackle fibers. Split the tails if you would like. Secure with a half hitch.

Step 2. Dub body to a point two eye-lengths from eye.

Step 3. Spin some dubbing on the thread into a ball big enough for the size fly you are tying. When you make a wrap, position the ball on top of the dubbing nearest the eye and tie down. Secure with a half hitch. If you need a bigger wing case, you can make a second ball and position it on top of the first ball. To make the ball, you need to spin the dubbing both directions on the thread—up and down—as well as spinning it around the thread.

Step 4. Dub around the ball and to the eye, tie off, and glue.

Searching for risers in the fog.

Hi Float Emerger

Back in the early years, when I was guiding or teaching, visibility was quite often a problem many of my clients experienced. They could not spot the fly as it drifted on the water or see the subtle rise when the trout made their move in a riffled run. To help combat this deficiency, we developed a cul-de-canard short wing on a fly tied like the Floating Nymph, which made it more visible. Also, teaching the customer how to put a slight movement in his or her fly by quickly tightening the bicep of the casting arm was not only helpful in spotting the fly but started the important teaching process of skittering.

HI FLOAT EMERGER MATERIALS

Hook standard dry fly hook

Thread 6/0

Tail gray cul-de-canard (CDC)

Body olive or brown dry fly dubbing (Gekko dubbing)

Wing light dun cul-de-canard trimmed off stem, brown fly-medium dun

HI FLOAT EMERGER TYING INSTRUCTIONS

Step 1. Tie in tail of cul-de-canard about three-quarters the length of the shank of the hook.

Step 2. Dub body to a point two eye-lengths from the eye.

Step 3. Cut some of the cul-de-canard off a few of the stems to use for wing. Tie in cul-de-canard. Lay a small bunch on the shank of the hook at the point where you stopped dubbing. Tie it down in the middle and fold the forward part back over the other; tie it down and secure with half hitch. Then trim the tips even. Dub over tie down and to eye, tie off, then glue.

Casting on a foggy morning.

MADAM X

For years, I wondered why rubber legs were never used in the construction of dry flies. So one night, when I was at my tying bench, I mounted two pair of white rubber legs on a size 10 dry fly hook. The fly had a large deer-hair wing, like a big caddis, and the legs were attached perpendicular to the shank.

The next day, I rushed up to Grayling and fished a couple miles downstream on Michigan's famous Au Sable River. The fishing was fair, but not as good as I had hoped. I went home and sat at my tying bench looking at my new creation, wondering how to improve it. The only thing that I could think of was to "X" the legs instead of having them stick straight out. I did that, and the rest is history. I went back to the Au Sable and had a fifty-fish day.

MADAM X MATERIALS

Hook standard dry fly hook

Thread 3/0

Tail & Body elk hair

Wing elk hair

Legs round rubber

MADAM X TYING INSTRUCTIONS

Step 1. Get the tips of the elk hair even by putting the hair in a stacker. Tie in the tail at a point just in front of the middle of the shank. Palmer the thread to the rear then back forward, forming Xs on the underside of the body. Tie down, then secure with a half hitch.

Step 2. Tie in underwing of elk hair at the point where you tied in the tail. Trim the butt ends of the elk off. Secure with half hitch.

Step 3. Tie in over wing, pointed forward. The overwing when pulled over should be the same length as the underwing, so measure it carefully as you have to allow for bending the hair. Wrap down the butt ends of the hair well so none will show on the underside of the fly. Secure with half hitch.

Step 4. Pull overwing back to form bullet head; tie down and secure with a half hitch. Tie in legs tightly to make them spread out and form an X. Make a half hitch at that point.

Step 5. Bring the thread forward under the fly and tie off at the eye, then glue.

Parachute Madam X

The obvious next step in development of the Madam X was the addition of parachute hackle, which not only improved floatation, but also increased durability and, more importantly, gave the pattern an entirely new look. In the mid-1980s, I introduced Parachute Madam X to Alaska at one of my schools. It was dynamite! Not only did it connect with dozens of big rainbows, mostly in the six- to ten-pound category, but it fooled many big silvers up to twenty pounds. According to the lodge owner, it was the first time he had witnessed large Pacific salmon caught on a dry fly. Up until a few years ago, when I finally stopped schooling in Alaska, the Parachute Madam X was responsible for catching dozens of big silvers.

The Parachute Madam X has become known all over most of the dry fly fishing world. You can find it in almost every fly shop. I never go fishing without some.

Carp on a Parachute Madam X.

PARACHUTE MADAM X MATERIALS

Hook standard dry fly hook

Thread monocord A

Abdomen thread

Tail & Wing elk

Thorax peacock herl

Post Antron

Hackle grizzly

Legs round rubber

PARACHUTE MADAM X TYING INSTRUCTIONS

Step 1. Tie in tail and body and wrap the colored monocord close together, making the abdomen the color you want.

Step 2. Tie in post and wing. Many people prefer to tie in the post before they tie in the wing, while others prefer to tie in the wing first. Do not skimp on the elk hair; it makes your fly float better if you have a good amount on the fly.

Step 3. Tie in herl, legs, and hackle. Here it gets a little confusing, but we feel this is the easiest way to continue. We tie in three pieces of herl, then we tie in the hackle, then the legs go in the middle. Wrap the thread on both sides of the post as you are tying in the legs, but keep the thread in the same place on the legs. Tie the legs in tightly so they X out properly and they do not pull out easily. Secure with a half hitch.

Step 4. Wrap the herl to front of legs. We use a hackle plier at that point to hold the herl so it does not unwrap.

Step 5. Wrap hackle and tie down. Secure with a half hitch. Use plenty of hackle for good floatation. Finish wrapping herl, tie off, and glue.

BUTTON FLY

The staple of my "match the hatch" box. These little guys have bailed me out of many difficult situations. They display a clean, simple outline to the trout. The Button has a parachute hackle locked down with our rubber post method. They float extremely well and are called Buttons because the rubber forms a perfectly round button when the post is clipped. They work dead drifting or skittering on rivers or lakes. We have great match-the-hatch colors.

BUTTON FLY MATERIALS

Hook standard dry fly hook

Thread 8/0

Tails cock hackle fibers

Body dry fly dubbing (color of your choice)

Post round rubber medium

Hackle light brown or color to match the fly you are imitating

BUTTON FLY TYING INSTRUCTIONS

Step 1. Tie in split tails. It is a good idea to put a little ball of dubbing on the hook just above the barb before you tie on the hackles, as it helps to split them and keep them split. Secure with a half hitch. Dub abdomen a little over halfway to the eye.

Step 2. Tie in rubber post and secure with half hitch, stretch it up, and attach it to your parachute tool. You do not have to stretch the rubber tight. Tie in hackle, then dub around the post and hackle tie in.

Step 3. Wrap several wraps of hackle and tie it down. Secure with a half hitch.

Step 4. Dub the thorax, tie off, then cut the rubber, leaving just a short stub. If you cut it too short, it will sink down into the hackle, and then the hackle will come loose. Tie off and glue.

Alternate view. Top view showing cut rubber post.

Double Parachute Hopper

This is one of our deadliest inventions. One of the most pleasurable and exciting forms of fly fishing occurs during the hopper season. In Montana, that is usually from about the middle of August until well into the fall. Some of the biggest trout of the year show up during this period.

Most anglers seem to definitely have their favorite pattern when it comes to these long-legged creatures, and there are so many. We would like to throw ours, the Double Parachute Hopper, in the hat. We know foam hoppers are very popular these days and that they work well, but give ours a try. It is a great floater, with a parachute at each end, very durable, easy to skitter, and it has a super pair of legs—and everyone likes great legs.

DOUBLE PARACHUTE HOPPER MATERIALS

Hook 2X long dry fly hook

Thread 6/0

Abdomen wool yarn or dry fly dubbing (color of your choice)

Rib heavy thread used for rod-building or monocord

Wing lacquered turkey quill

Legs pheasant tail fibers (knotted)

Front Post white calf tail

Rear Post round rubber (small or medium)

Rear Hackle grizzly

Front Hackle brown and grizzly

Thorax the color of dubbing you choose for your hopper

DOUBLE PARACHUTE HOPPER TYING INSTRUCTIONS

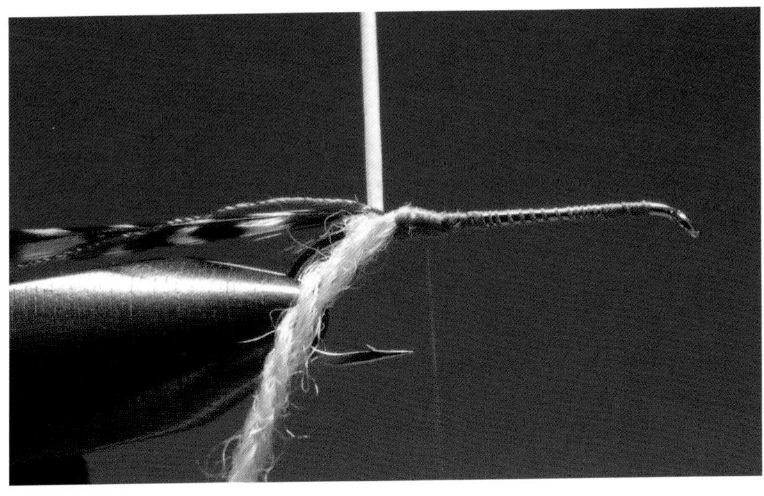

Step 1. Tie in ribbing and rear rubber post. Secure with a half hitch. Tie in hackle (about a size 16) and the wool yarn. Just leave it all hanging for now. It sounds like a lot in one spot, but it works out the best.

Step 2. Attach the rubber to your parachute tool, stretching it—but not real tight. Then wrap the hackle and tie it down. Secure with a half hitch. Tie in front post of calf tail, tie it down, and secure with a half hitch. Wrap the yarn to the front post and secure. Wrap the ribbing to the front post and tie down.

Step 3. Cut the rubber post, leaving just a little stub. Tie in wing securely right in back of the front post. Secure with a half hitch. Tie in legs tightly, wrapping the thread in front of the post as well as in back of the post. Secure with a half hitch. Then trim off the butts of the fibers of the legs and tie them down. Dub around tie in of legs and wing and wrap some dubbing under the legs to help hold them out away from the body.

Step 4. Tie in the hackle. Secure with a half hitch.

Step 5. Wrap the hackle, tie down, and secure with a half hitch and dub to the eye. Tie off fly and glue. Glue knots on legs also.

Alternate view. Top view.

Brownie delight.

SPECKL-X

Another one of our "X" dry flies that was deadly for big browns, especially at our schools and presentations in both New Zealand and Chile. We could hardly keep the fish off it when we fished the Bow River in Canada. They actually torpedoed up out of the water to grab it. Also, this pattern, tied on a saltwater hook and adding a little bit of extra hackle, was deadly when we were fishing the backcountry of South Florida for snook, jacks, redfish, and even small tarpon. This pattern has the advantage of great visibility, because the fluff of the grizzly hackle is left on when the parachute hackle is applied. Unfortunately, other critters relish this creation. We've hooked a few gators over the years.

SPECKL-X MATERIALS

Hook 2X long dry fly hook

Thread 3/0 brown

Tail & Wing elk hair

Abdomen yarn or tan dry fly dubbing

Thorax tan dry fly dubbing

Post round rubber

Legs speckled round rubber

Hackle brown and grizzly (grizzly with the fluff on the bottom)

SPECKL-X TYING INSTRUCTIONS

Step 1. Tie in tail of elk hair at a point two-thirds of the way to the eye of the hook. Make the tail about the length of the gap of the hook. Wrap the thread back to a point right over the barb. Tie in the yarn and secure with a half hitch.

Step 2. Wrap the yarn and tie it down at the point where you tied in the tail. Palmer your thread back to just above the barb and then forward to form Xs on the bottom of the abdomen. Tie down and secure with a half hitch. Tie in the wing so it is the same length as the tail after you stack the tips so they are even in a hair stacker. Secure with a half hitch. Tie in the rubber post firmly, at the point where you tied in the wing. Secure with a half hitch. Stretch the rubber post up to your parachute tool and secure.

Step 3. Tie in the speckled rubber legs fairly tightly so they will form an X. Secure with a half hitch. Then tie in the hackle securely, making sure you have the grizzly hackle with the fluff on the top of the brown hackle when you tic it in. Dub around where you tied in the legs and hackle.

Step 4. Wrap the brown hackle first and secure with hackle pliers. Then make a couple wraps on top of the brown hackle with the grizzly hackle so the fluff is at the top of the parachute. Wrap the grizzly hackle down through the brown hackle and tie off. Secure with a half hitch and dub the thorax.

Step 5. Tie off. Then cut the rubber post, leaving a little stub so the rubber does not sink down into the hackle. If the rubber sinks down into the hackle, it will come unwound. Glue the tie off and place a spot of glue where the legs are tied in.

Alternate view. Bottom of fly shows Xs on abdomen.

Para-Tractor

This is a dynamite new series of attractor dry flies that utilizes our rubber post method of attaching the parachute hackle. The rubber locks in the hackle feathers, making a high-floating fly that is extremely durable and easy to skitter. I always carry these in tan and olive. We have had amazing fishing on the Missouri and Bitterroot Rivers with these flies, midsummer.

PARA-TRACTOR MATERIALS

Hook standard dry fly hook

Thread 6/0

Tail good quality hackle fibers

Abdomen dry fly dubbing (color of your choice)

Post round rubber and white Phentex or Antron

Hackle grizzly or your choice

PARA-TRACTOR TYING INSTRUCTIONS

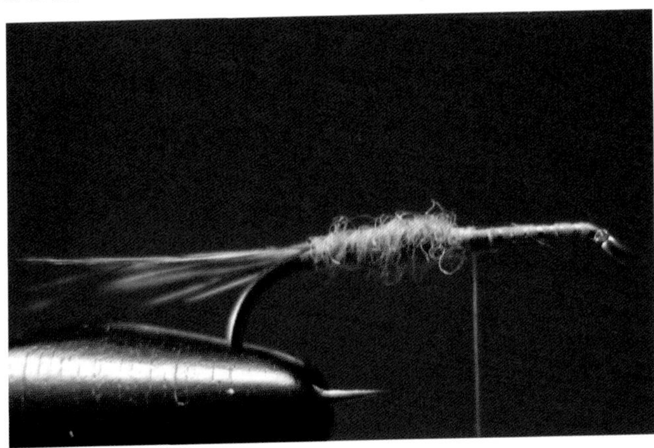

Step 1. Tie in the tail of good quality hackle and secure with a half hitch. Dub the abdomen to the middle of the hook.

Step 2. Tie in rubber post firmly. Secure with a half hitch. Then connect the rubber to your parachute tool. Tie in the Phentex post, sliding it all around the rubber post. Make several wraps of thread around the post to hold the Phentex in place. Secure with a half hitch. Dub around the post's tie in.

Step 3. Tie in the hackle and dub around tie in.

Step 4. Wrap hackle, making sure the Phentex still goes all around the rubber post. Tie down the hackle and secure with a half hitch. Now dub the thorax and tie off the fly.

Step 5. Cut rubber, leaving a short stub. If you cut it too short, it will sink down into the hackle and you will lose your hackle. Glue tie off.

HARE & HERL

This yummy-looking parachute with a peacock herl body, grizzly hackle, and snowshoe rabbit post and tail floats extremely well and is easy to see on the water. In the smaller sizes, it looks amazingly like a trico dun. In fact, on the Bighorn River, it substitutes beautifully for the extra-large species that blankets the water from August until mid-October. If you are fishing the hopper-dropper system, it makes a great choice as the tail end pattern. Even up in the reservoir above the dam, the Hare & Herl is deadly when fishing for those selectively rising carp. Angling for those big boys is a real blast, in case you have not tried it. Be sure not to set your hooks too quickly, as you will miss every time.

HARE & HERL MATERIALS

Hook standard dry fly hook

Thread 6/0 or 8/0

Tail snowshoe rabbit

Body peacock herl

Post snowshoe rabbit

Hackle grizzly

HARE & HERL TYING INSTRUCTIONS

Step 1. Tie in tail and post of snowshoe rabbit. Just cut little clumps off the rabbit foot the length you think you need them. Remember to wrap your thread around the post several times when you tie it in so it will stand up straight.

Step 2. Tie in herl. I use three pieces on the size 12. Wrap herl to the post and secure with hackle pliers. It helps to twist the herl together as you wrap.

Step 3. Tie in hackle at the base of the post and bring herl forward over where you tied in hackle.

Step 4. Wrap the hackle at least five or six wraps to help floatation.

Step 5. Finish wrapping the herl to the eye and tie down. Tie off the fly. Put a little glue along the bottom of the herl to strengthen the herl. Tie off the fly and glue.

Dancing Caddis

This is one of our signature dry flies that has become very popular all over Montana, especially with the guides. Since parachutes have become so popular, everyone wants a white post. These dancers are undoubtedly our best caddis imitation; they float like a cork, skitter beautifully, and are easy to spot on the water and very durable. I don't go anywhere without them in my box. We have even tied them in a large size for a motorboat caddis imitation.

DANCING CADDIS MATERIALS

Hook standard dry fly hook

Thread 6/0

Body good dry fly dubbing

Wing elk hair

Post Phentex or Antron

Hackle brown and grizzly

DANCING CADDIS TYING INSTRUCTIONS

Step 1. Dub body two-thirds of the way to the eye. Tie in a wing of elk hair after you have evened the tips in a stacker. Make the wing about the length of the gap of the hook past the bend. Tie it down and secure with a half hitch.

Step 2. Tie in the post over the tie in of the wing and dub around it.

Step 3. Tie in hackle and secure with a half hitch, then wrap it and tie it down securely. Secure with a half hitch. Dub to the eye and tie off, then glue.

Releasing the big one.

CLUMPA

One of our most popular dry flies over the past few years has been the Clumpa, mainly due to its versatility. Simply put, it seems to work under most any condition—hatches, spinner falls, caddis egg laying—and as an attractor, even during those periods when nothing is on the water. I always carry a handful in my general fly-fishing box. And we tie them in so many colors and sizes: black, olive, gray, yellow, sulphur, purple, and from size 12 down to size 18.

Quite often, I fish a bunch of them, usually four or five, creating my own little hatch. I tie them in a straight line, going from the eye to the bend of the next hook, and keep the cast mended so it stays perpendicular to the current. If you use more than three flies in the system, it gets a little tricky to cast, but that's why we practice. You can use any fly for this setup, but I use the Clumpa because it floats so well, is easy to maneuver, and works great.

CLUMPA MATERIALS

Hook standard dry fly hook

Thread 8/0

Tails cock hackle fibers

Body dry fly dubbing (color of your choice)

Post round rubber (medium)

Hackle grizzly or your choice

CLUMPA TYING INSTRUCTIONS

Step 1. Tie in split tails. Put a small ball of dubbing on the shank just above the barb, as it helps split the tails and keeps them split. Secure with a half hitch.

Step 2. Dub abdomen a little over halfway to eye. Tie in rubber post, secure with a half hitch, and stretch the rubber up to your parachute tool. Do not stretch it too tight.

Step 3. Tie in hackle and dub around where you have tied in the post and hackle.

Step 4. Wrap the hackle up the post to a point equal to the distance from the post to just before the eye, then wrap it back down and tie down. Secure with a half hitch.

Step 5. Finish dubbing to a point about one eye-length before the eye. Take your finger and thumb and hold the hackle on the post back so you can lay the post and hackle on the top of the dubbed thorax without catching a lot of hackle between. Remove the rubber post from your parachute tool. Lay post and hackle on top of the thorax, pulling it forward so the hackle is just behind the eye, and tie down the rubber post at the point one eye-length from eye. Tie it down securely with a half hitch. Cut off excess rubber and tie down the rubber stub. Dub the tie down, tie off the fly, and glue.

TIGER TAIL

I love fishing on Montana's premier trout lake, Georgetown, mainly because the hatches are heavy and the fish are so energetic. I would rather catch a fifteen-inch lake rainbow than a twenty-incher from any stream you can name. It is all in the food source. The lake is loaded with damsels and dragonflies, not to mention the super hatches of *Baetis*, *Callibaetis*, motorboat caddis, and an abundance of minnows and scud. The streams cannot begin to match this volume of food. Also, Georgetown Lake is loaded with weedbeds that grow to the surface most of the year. This means lots of dry fly fishing is mandatory a good portion of the season.

This situation gave rise to the creation of the Tiger Tail dry fly and what I call the *knock knock* fishing system. With this technique, aim your casting loop so the fly slaps the water surface, creating a fish attracting commotion, not just once, at least twice, and sometimes three times: *knock, knock, knock*. I have released hundreds of fish, normally good size ones, using the *knock knock*.

The Tiger Tail is perfect for this technique, with its incredible floatation and skittering qualities. Actually, I have used the *knock knock* for huge bass in Florida and monster pike in Alaska. Also, back in the 1980s, right after Perma Float tying hooks came on the market, I tied the original Tiger Tails on these molded plastic hooks, which of course floated like corks. This, in my opinion, was probably one of the greatest fly-tying developments in my lifetime. Unfortunately, they went out of business.

TIGER TAIL MATERIALS

Hook standard dry fly hook

Thread 6/0

Tail Phentex yarn and grizzly hackle #18

Body dry fly dubbing

Post round rubber

Wing grizzly hackle #12

TIGER TAIL TYING INSTRUCTIONS

Step 1. Tie in Phentex yarn and stretch to parachute tool. Tie in grizzly hackle, then palmer up the yarn about three-quarters of an inch and back down. Then tie down the hackle and secure with a half hitch.

Step 2. Dub the abdomen with good dry fly dubbing to a point about halfway to the eye. Tie in the round rubber for the post. Secure with a half hitch.

Step 3. Secure rubber post to parachute tool. Tie in the hackle.

Step 4. Wrap the hackle up the post the same distance from the post to a point one eye-length before the eye of the hook. Wrap back down and tie down the hackle. Secure with a half hitch.

Step 5. Dub the thorax to a point just before the eye. Take your finger and thumb and hold the hackle on the post back so you can lay the post and hackle on the top of the dubbed thorax without catching a lot of hackle between. Remove the rubber post from your parachute tool. Lay post and hackle on top of the thorax, pulling it forward so the hackle is just behind the eye, and tie down the rubber post at the point one eye-length from eye. Tie it down securely with a half hitch. Cut off excess rubber and tie down the rubber stub. Dub the tie down, tie off the fly, and glue.

Nymphs and Strymphs

The dramatic explosion of fly-tying materials over the past few years, especially our new action dubbing, has greatly contributed to the development of great nymph and "strymph" patterns, with the emphasis on synthetics. This is good news to the animals of the world, as their numbers are constantly being pressured. Also, man's plastic imitations, in most cases, are more durable and attract more attention. Many are either perfectly round or trilobal in shape, stretchy in texture, and translucent, glow-in-the-dark, or ultraviolet in color.

THE STORY OF OUR ACTION DUBBING

My first attempt at tying flies was way back in the mid-1950s, right after I got out of the service. I had a couple of good tutors, Carl Richards and Ernie Schwiebert. Not that I began to approach their degree of efficiency, but it was great to have such good teachers. Back in those days, the most popular dubbing available was rabbit. To keep my cost down, I asked my hunting friends to save all the bunny tails for me. Then I would dye them all the various basic colors—olive, brown, yellow, et cetera—and, if you're familiar with rabbit rumps, you would get quite a variety of shades from dark on top to light on bottom. That way, I would get every color in the rainbow, saving the expense of buying so many packs of dubbing.

For almost forty years, the dubbing market changed very little, which is quite surprising. There were drastic developments in other fly-fishing products, like rods, reels, lines, and what I call "shiny" fly-tying products, such as Krystal Flash and glow-in-the-dark materials.

Soon after the original edition of *Selective Trout* was published, Carl and I started thinking about the possibility of mixing the legs right in with the dubbing. I remember many occasions sitting up all night in his cabin on the North Branch of the Au Sable River trying to figure out how to do it. Unfortunately, he passed on, losing the most talented combination tier/angler the world of fly fishing has ever seen.

I thought my quest for "legs in the dubbing" was over. When I moved to Montana and got acquainted with Doug Brewer, undoubtedly the most knowledgeable individual about fly-tying materials I have ever met. He lives right up the road from me here in Western Montana. Plus, he is a fantastic flytier and throws one of the prettiest loops you will ever see. Oh, I almost forgot, he had all the equipment, and know-how, to make the dubbing we need. In 2000, we mixed up the first batch of dubbing with legs using sheared rabbit and rubber mini legs. This became known as Rub-A-Dub dubbing. The following year, the next generation was rabbit with rubber microlegs and was called Generation X dubbing. A couple years later, Peacock Plus was invented using synthetic legs, which we call Wigglys, resulting in a peacock-looking material.

A few months later, the combination of two sizes of legs with a peacock-style dubbing was born. It is called Peacock Plus Big Daddy. Then, by combining six different colors of legs, we developed a gorgeous dubbing we call Super Mix. And then came our very popular dubbing called Generation X-Treme. Over the next couple years, in quick succession, Doug Brewer came out with Triple Threat, SSS,

Sea Dragon, Mega dubbing, and a new one called Kraken dubbing. All of these have different length and color of Wigglys. We carry all of these on our website.

The addition of legs gives more movement than dubbing with dubbing fibers only. The action of the legs in still water is very noticeable. It comes alive instantly. The contrasting leg colors, and even the matching leg colors, enhance and change the overall color appearance of the base dubbing. It is that much more visible in the water. You can change the color appearance of the dubbing with the addition of different leg colors. It can be very dramatic and exciting!

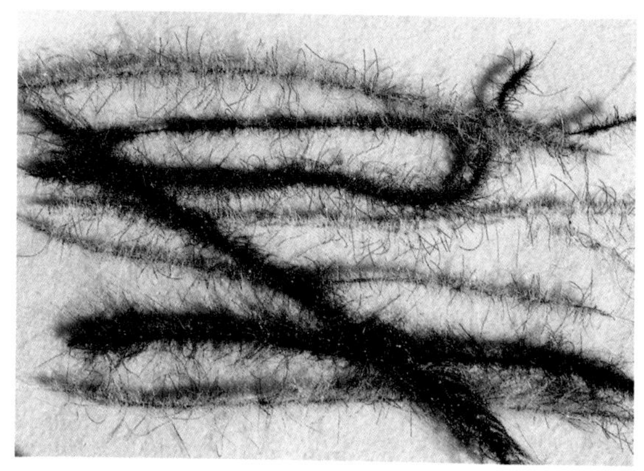

Dubbing brushes made of Rub-A-Dub dubbing.

These styles of dubbing are easy to use; you can dub by hand, dubbing loop, dubbing brushes, or stack dubbing. Using the dubbing with longer legs can eliminate the use of saddle hackle and chenille on woolly bugger–style flies, with the added bonus of durability and the unlimited color combinations of legs and dubbing within each fly. Action dubbing also makes superb tails on nymphs and streamers, as the movement is outstanding, and it makes Matuka- and Zonker-style flies with different colors of leg and dubbing on the same fly. Color combinations are endless.

Articulated flies are much more practical to tie with these types of dubbing. Back in the late 1960s and 1970s, Carl and I tied them for steelhead, large trout, and pike. All we had was marabou, schlappen, herl, and a few other natural materials. Not only did those flies lack durability, but they really did not have the action the new dubbings have. The new Wigglys have incredible movement in the water!

One of the most important advantages of the action dubbings is that they make incredible brushes. The sky is the limit. You can mix different types of materials (both natural and synthetic), lengths of fibers, colors, textures, and it makes the most durable concoction you will ever see in a fly. They are absolutely dynamite for steelhead, pike, bass, saltwater, and big trout.

These types of dubbing open up a whole new world of fly tying and fly fishing to all flytiers and fly fishers alike. It is not narrowly focused on a certain fly size or type of tying.

Another great Montana rainbow.

Rub-A-Dub Nymph

These were the very first flies made out of our new action dubbing that Doug Brewer made for us back in 2000. Doug, known in the fly-tying world as the "Mad Scientist," is undoubtedly the premier expert on materials and one of the best tiers on the planet. The new dubbings were made of both natural and synthetic fibers and came in great nymphal colors: a combination of black, olive, brown, and gray. These original flies were made from tiny brushes, with the dubbing only about one-half of an inch in diameter and Wigglys protruding out, making the brush about one inch or more in diameter. This created an unbelievable action in the water that fish found hard to resist. We tested these nymphs here in Montana and on both the north and south islands of New Zealand and found them to be dynamite everywhere.

RUB-A-DUB NYMPH MATERIALS

Hook standard nymph hook

Weight gold bead

Thread 8/0

Wing Case scud back

Tail Rub-A-Dub Wigglys

Body Rub-A-Dub nymph dubbing brush

RUB-A-DUB NYMPH TYING INSTRUCTIONS

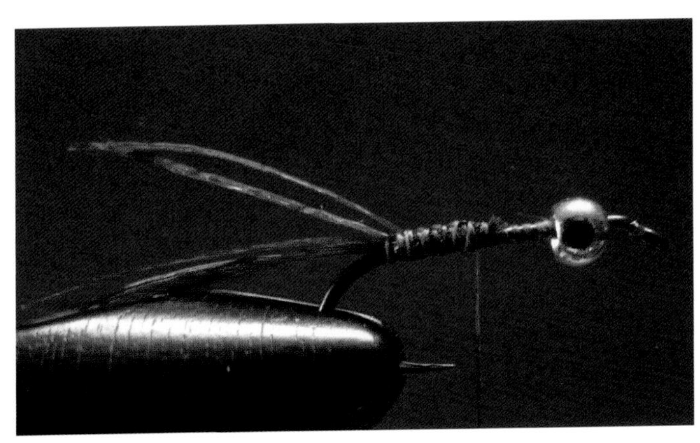

Step 1. Place bead on hook. Tie in a few strands of Wiggly hackle for a tail. We usually grab a few strands, lay them on top of the shank of the hook about one-third of the way toward the eye, make a few wraps in the middle to tie them in, then fold them back and tie them down. You can cut off any excess. Wrap your thread back to the barb. Secure with a half hitch.

Step 2. At that point above the barb, tie in the Rub-A-Dub dubbing brush. Secure with a half hitch.

Step 3. Wrap the dubbing brush two-thirds of the way to the eye, brushing the Wigglys back with a Velcro brush as you wrap. (Make a Velcro brush by gluing a piece of Velcro on a tongue depressor.) Make a few wraps to secure. Then tie in the scud back. Secure with a half hitch.

Step 4. Finish wrapping the brush to eye, tie it down, and secure with a half hitch. Pull forward and secure the scud back, then tie off. Brush the fly with a Velcro brush and glue tie off.

Identical twins.

Rub-A-Dub Strymph

A couple miles downstream from one of my favorite towns (Gore, New Zealand) is a run on the Mataura River that is billed as the best brown trout water in the world. I do not know if that is true or not, but it sure seemed to be back in the 1980s and 1990s when we were doing our schools in Kiwiland. This run has a gravel pit on it, and on the south bank is a beautifully wooded area with lots of branches hanging out over the water. Depending on the water level and time of the year, you had to make quite a long cast, seventy to eighty feet, to cover the fish properly, most of which were browns well over twenty inches.

Occasionally, one of those big boys would dash out and grab a Rub-A-Dub Nymph or small dry fly, but it usually required lots of repetitive casting. We bumped up our Rub-A-Dub to a small streamer size, better known as "strymphs," and our luck changed drastically. We also made the Wigglys longer, which greatly increased the action. The Montana fish, trout, bass, and pike also really like the new style of movement and gyrations.

RUB-A-DUB STRYMPH MATERIALS

Hook 3X long streamer hook

Weight gold bead

Thread 6/0

Tail Rub-A-Dub Wigglys

Body strymph dubbing brush

RUB-A-DUB STRYMPH TYING INSTRUCTIONS

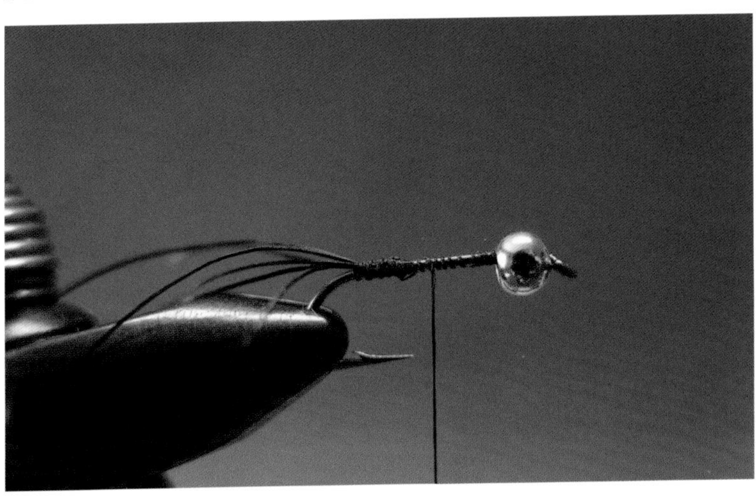

Step 1. Place bead on hook. Tie in a few strands of Wigglys for a tail. Lay the Wigglys on top of the shank about a quarter of an inch from the barb, wrap your thread around the middle, and fold the front half back over the others and tie down. Wrap your thread back to a point just above the barb. Secure with half hitch.

Step 2. Tie in the strymph dubbing brush above the barb. Secure with half hitch.

Step 3. Wrap the dubbing brush to the eye, brushing it back with your Velcro brush. Tie down and cut off the brush with old scissors. Add a few strands of Wigglys around the bead to give the fly more action at the front. Brush the fly again with a Velcro brush and trim any Wigglys that are too long, then glue.

Skinny Minnie, but long!

Georgie Boy

Tying a Georgie Boy is about as simple as fly tying gets, but do not be fooled by the lack of skill required to tie the pattern. We have caught dozens and dozens of fish on this little guy, not only trout, but salmon, steelhead, pike, bass, carp, and saltwater species. The reason it works so well, I think, is the material used to create it, which is Generation X, one of our top-selling action dubbings. A little tip we use in tying for ourselves is to add 20 percent to 30 percent more Wigglys. Then, after you brush out the dubbing with your Velcro brush, you won't believe the action when you cast the fly in the water. That is why you can simply make the cast and just let the fly lay on the bottom. We have caught hundreds of fish using this "no technique" system.

GEORGIE BOY MATERIALS

Hook 3X long streamer hook

Bead black to match hook size

Thread 6/0

Dubbing Generation X dubbing (olive with extra short black Wigglys)

GEORGIE BOY TYING INSTRUCTIONS

Step 1. Place bead on hook. We add some extra black Generation X Wigglys to the olive dubbing so we have more Wigglys in the body. Dub the whole body of the fly, from just above the barb to the bead, but do not twist the dubbing tight. You will want to use a high-tack wax, as this dubbing with the Wigglys in it is a little harder to dub; but when you brush out those Wigglys, the action is unbelievable.

Step 2. Tie off fly and glue. Then brush out Wigglys with Velcro brush or a piece of Velcro.

Georgie Long Legs

This is one of my all-time favorite, go-to trout flies. I believe the reason it is so deadly is the tremendous total action it has in the water. All the parts are moving (Wigglys in the body and tail and long rubber legs that gyrate on the retrieve). It undoubtedly has more action than any other pattern in my fly box. We had a hard time naming it, not knowing whether to put it in the strymph or streamer category. We finally decided to call it a strymph, but it does not matter what it is called. It works really well in both rivers and lakes, especially in places like Alaska, New Zealand, South Africa, and here in Montana.

GEORGIE LONG LEGS MATERIALS

Hook 3X long streamer hook

Bead black to match hook size

Thread 6/0

Legs Incredible Legs

Dubbing olive Generation X

Tail black Generation X Wigglys

GEORGIE LONG LEGS TYING INSTRUCTIONS

Step 1. Place bead on hook. Tie in Incredible Legs on the underside of the hook. Wrap the thread around the legs like you would dumbbell eyes, making the legs point forward. Secure with a half hitch.

Step 2. Tie in tail of Generation X Wigglys about half to three-quarters of an inch long. It is easier to grab a little bunch and tie it on in the middle and fold them back over themselves and tie down. You can always cut them off if you get too many or they are longer than you want. Secure with a half hitch.

Step 3. We add some extra black Generation X Wigglys to the olive dubbing so we have more Wigglys in the body. Dub body of the fly with the Generation X dubbing from just above barb, around the legs, and to the bead. You may want to use some high-tack wax, as the Wigglys don't always want to stay on the thread. But if you do, make sure to not wrap the dubbing on the thread too tight. Tie off and brush out Wigglys with Velcro brush or a piece of Velcro, then glue.

Rainbow from the headwater of our local lake.

Mono Caddis Pupa

In the extreme southern part of Chile, there are massive numbers of small- to medium-sized caddis that are found mostly in the super clear rivers and the blue-water mountain lakes. Hatches usually start late in the afternoon and continue well into the evening. The pupas are bright green, almost chartreuse, and leisurely swim to the surface, where they literally explode into the adult phase and quickly fly away. They are available to the trout for a much longer period of time than the fully grown fly, which is similar to our Rhyacophilidae with a green body and speckled gray wing. To match the bright green color of the pupa, we use chartreuse monofilament, attached to the hook like you would tie off a fly.

Fish the fly with a rising motion, twitching it as you retrieve. We have found this pupa works well in many areas of the United States. We have them in our box wherever we go when there are caddis out.

MONO CADDIS PUPA MATERIALS

Hook scud hook

Thread 6/0

Bead gold

Body green monofilament

Thorax Generation X dubbing, black

MONO CADDIS PUPA TYING INSTRUCTIONS

Step 1. Place bead on hook and attach monofilament to the hook by doing a hand whip finish. Starting at a point above the barb, do about sixteen wraps.

Step 2. Tie on thread at the point where you quit, making wraps with the monofilament. Apply some wax to the thread and make a dubbing noodle, not tightly spun.

Step 3. Wrap the dubbing to the eye of the hook. Tie down and glue. Brush dubbing with your Velcro brush or a piece of Velcro to bring out the Wigglys. This gives the fly a lot of action.

Searching for risers at sunset.

DIVA NYMPH

Back in 2002 when Generation X-Treme dubbing was developed, we had fun tying new flies and testing them. The materials in the dubbing are all synthetic and loaded with Generation X Wigglys mixed in. These are our smallest size of Wigglys (.002), and using this dubbing for the wing and legs of a nymph gives it serious action most nymphs in previous years did not have. We tied and tested many nymphs and strymphs. We finally decided to go with the Diva Nymph for the website, even though several other nymphs we tested worked well. It has a black bead, and the abdomen is body wrap, which gives it the segmented natural look of a nymph. The fish on the Missouri and Big Hole Rivers seemed to like the Diva quite well. These two rivers are great for testing flies, besides our local river, the Bitterroot. Both are only about three and a half hours from where we live. We tie this nymph in sizes 14, 16, and 18, which are good sizes for the hopper-dropper setup as well.

DIVA NYMPH MATERIALS

Hook standard nymph hook

Bead black brass

Thread 8/0

Tail Generation X Wigglys

Abdomen body wrap

Wing Case stretch tubing

Wing Generation X dubbing

DIVA NYMPH TYING INSTRUCTIONS

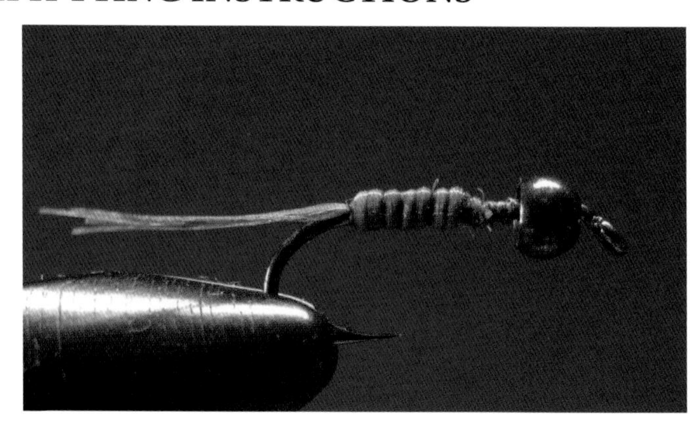

Step 1. Place the black bead on hook. Tie in a few strands of Generation X Wigglys for a tail. Tie in body wrap and wrap it to a point a little forward of the middle of the shank of the hook and tie down. Secure with half hitch.

Step 2. Tie in stretch tubing for wing case. Secure with half hitch.

Step 3. Put some dubbing wax on the thread and make a dubbing noodle. Do not wrap the dubbing too tight, as you have to brush out the Wigglys in the dubbing with a piece of Velcro or a Velcro brush. Wrap the thread with dubbing forward to bead and tie down.

Step 4. Pull the stretch tubing forward and tie it down at the bead. Tie off the fly and glue, then brush the fly with your Velcro brush.

Alternate view. Picture shows top of fly.

Damsel Nymph

Georgetown Lake is a pristine body of water located in central Montana and is one of our favorite places to go fishing. It has an incredible damselfly hatch, turning the shoreline what we call *damsel blue* in late June when the emergence begins. Over the years, there have been dozens of patterns designed to imitate this monster hatch, but none have had any degree of consistency. We tied and tested several different imitations. Like so many others, we used marabou. However, our fly consists of a very slim body, like the natural, with some olive wire, as well as small, bead chain eyes. We tested our damsel pattern at Georgetown and a couple other small lakes and were pleased at the results.

DAMSEL NYMPH MATERIALS

Hook 3X long streamer hook

Thread 6/0 olive

Eyes x-small

Tail, Abdomen, Thorax marabou

Ribbing olive wire

DAMSEL NYMPH TYING INSTRUCTIONS

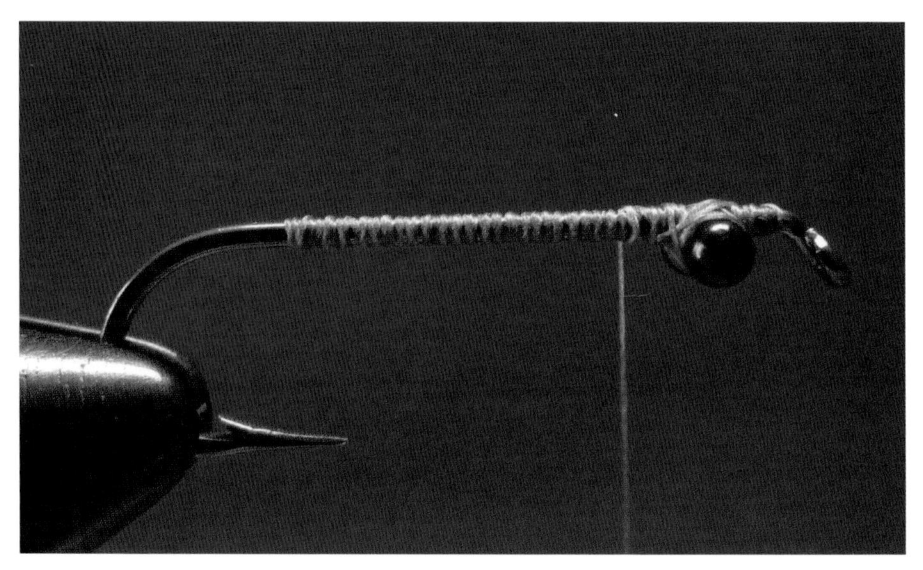

Step 1. Tie bead chain eyes on the underside of hook a little more than one eye-length from eye.

Step 2. Tie in olive wire above the barb, then tie in tips of some long fibers of marabou at the same point as the wire to make a tail about one-half inch long. Secure with a half hitch.

Step 3. Twist the marabou and wrap forward going over the eyes and tie down. Secure with a half hitch. You will have to keep twisting lightly as you wrap the marabou.

Step 4. Wrap the olive wire forward, side by side to the eye, and tie down. Secure with a half hitch. Add a few fibers of marabou behind the eyes a little less than half an inch long. Tie off the fly and glue.

A side-by-side comparison of a GID fly in natural light and glowing in the dark.

Glow-in-the-Dark Nymph

While giving demos in New Zealand a few years ago, we noticed an abundance of glow-in-the-dark fly-tying products in all the fly shops. When we got back home to Montana, we decided not only to get involved with glow-in-the-dark materials, but also the flies. In our area, we have numerous lakes with both trout and bass. This nymph, with the extreme glow in the wing case as well as the rest of the body, is one of our favorite patterns, especially in the deeper holes and pockets. It's also a great late-season pattern on the Beaverhead and Big Hole Rivers. To make sure the flies always have a bright glow, I carry a tiny camera flash in my pocket. Many people believe glow-in-the-dark means you have to fish at night; however, these flies work well during the day also. On a sunny day, try putting the nymph on your vest for a few minutes before you fish it so the sun can charge it.

GLOW-IN-THE-DARK NYMPH MATERIALS

Hook standard nymph hook, size 10 or 12

Bead chartreuse glass

Thread florescent yellow ultra thread

Tail glow-in-the-dark Flashabou

Abdomen glow-in-the-dark super floss

Wing Case glow-in-the-dark tape

Thorax cut-up pieces of glow-in-the-dark Flashabou (mixed colors)

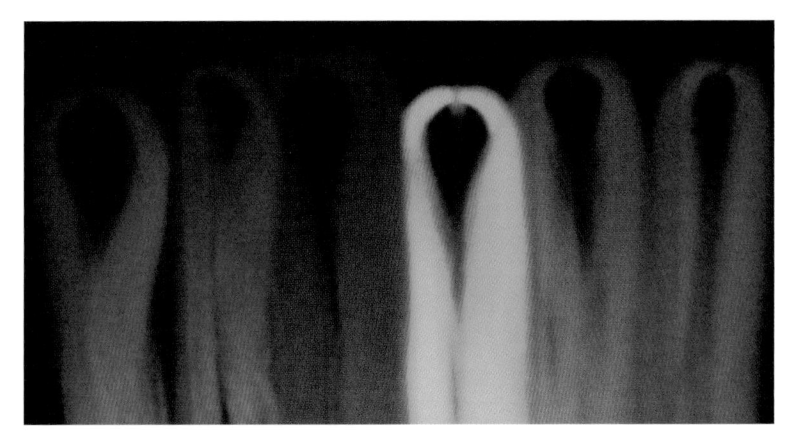

Close-up of glow-in-the-dark fibers.

GLOW-IN-THE-DARK NYMPH TYING INSTRUCTIONS

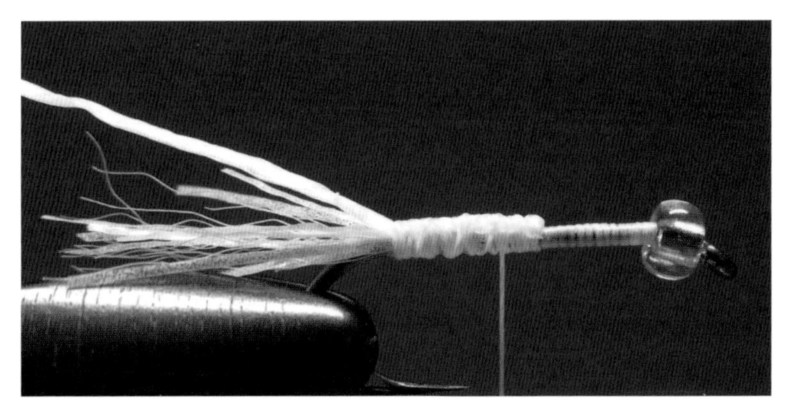

Step 1. Place glass bead on hook, tie in tail about a half inch long of glow-in-the-dark Flashabou, then tie in glow-in-the-dark super floss. Secure with a half hitch.

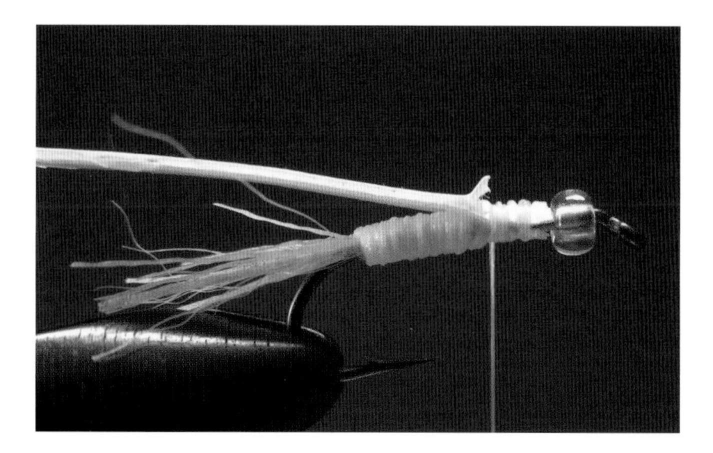

Step 2. Wrap the super floss to a point just past the center of the hook. Tie in glow-in-the-dark tape for wing case. Secure with a half hitch. The glow-in-the-dark tape you can normally find at hardware stores. Just cut a thin strip off, remove a small amount of the backing, and tie it in. Secure with a half hitch. It is very sticky, so leave the backing on while you are wrapping the dubbing.

Step 3. Put a high-tack wax on the thread and stick the cut-up Flashabou to the thread. Wrap it around the shank of the hook, tying the Flashabou on like you would dubbing. You may have to stick more on several times until you get to the bead. Pull off the rest of the backing on the glow-in-the-dark tape and pull the tape forward over the Flashabou and tie it down. Tie off the fly and glue. The pieces of Flashabou will stick out all over like the Wigglys on the Diva Nymph.

Alternate view. Back glowing.

Alternate view. Side glowing.

VX Nymph

In 2015, with the big popularity of ultraviolet, we decided to try some. Doug Brewer, the "Mad Scientist" who makes our action dubbing, was interested in trying it also. So he made several different kinds of ultraviolet dubbing: some with Wigglys and some without; some with long and short Wigglys with enhancer; and some with just short Wigglys with enhancer. His line of ultraviolet products is called UV-X and is one of the best in the business. We immediately started tying flies and testing them. It surprised us how well the fish ate them. Because the dubbing with the small Wigglys in it works so well on nymphs, we tied a nymph similar to the Diva, as well as some other ultraviolet flies, and went fishing. They all caught fish, but the nymph was dynamite. We added it to our line of flies, calling it the VX Nymph.

VX NYMPH MATERIALS

Hook 2X long nymph hook

Bead black brass

Thread 6/0 brown

Tail UV-X Wigglys

Underbody brown Generation X dubbing

Ribbing ultraviolet stretch tubing

Wing Case ultraviolet scud back

Thorax UV-X dubbing with legs

VX NYMPH TYING INSTRUCTIONS

Step 1. Put black bead on hook. At a point right above the barb, tie on tail of a few strands of UV-X Wigglys, then tie on some stretch tubing.

Step 2. Dub brown Generation X dubbing just past the middle of the hook. Wrap the stretch tubing over the brown dubbing to the point where you stopped dubbing. You do not have to wrap the tubing so that it is touching the last wrap; we want to leave a little space between wraps.

Step 3. Tie in scud back where you stopped dubbing, apply some dubbing wax to the thread, and make a dubbing noodle. Do not wrap the dubbing on too tight, as you are going to brush out the Wigglys with a piece of Velcro or a Velcro brush. Wrap the dubbing to the bead.

Step 4. Pull the scud back to the bead, tie it down, and tie off the fly. Brush the thorax with a piece of Velcro or a Velcro brush to pull out some of the Wigglys in the dubbing. This gives the fly a lot of action. Glue tie off.

Alternate view. The VX Nymph under ultraviolet light.

Streamers

Years ago, back in the early 1960s, I started giving casting presentations and schools in Alaska and all over the United States. A good share of my fishing was done with a streamer, quite often with a muddler. This is still one of my favorites, only my present-day version is ultraviolet-activated. By 1970, I expanded my demonstrations and schools to pretty much all over the world. In 1979, Sharon and I began giving clinics in places like Alaska, New Zealand, Chile, and numerous other countries. If the fish are not rising, we love to fish streamers. Today, we have streamers to which we have added extra Wigglys. Our action dubbing, glow-in-the-dark, and ultraviolet also give them more action.

Girdle Bugger

Devil Leech

Rub-A-Dub Streamer

All Black

Mantilla

Veil Fly

Little Ripper

Eradicator

Glitzy Legs

A trout caught with the Eradicator.

Girdle Bugger

The Girdle Bugger was our first streamer with rubber legs, and it also featured a yellow marabou tail. When we used it on the Bighorn River over twenty years ago, it was dynamite. We shared some with our fly-fishing friends, who gave one to a guide. The pattern became an instant success. When we returned the following year, it had become the most popular streamer on the river. Usually there is a reason why a fly would gain so much popularity as quickly as the Girdle Bugger did, but in this case we don't know why—it just did. Although, a few years ago, the Girdle Bugger was responsible for the biggest trout I have ever caught in Montana. When we are floating, we cast the Girdle Bugger tight to the bank and strip it at a rather quick pace.

GIRDLE BUGGER MATERIALS

Hook streamer 3X long

Weight lead wire .020

Bead gold

Tail yellow marabou

Legs yellow round rubber (medium)

Body yellow and brown variegated chenille

GIRDLE BUGGER TYING INSTRUCTIONS

Step 1. Put gold bead on hook. Wrap 16 wraps of lead wire on the shank of the hook. Leave about two eye-lengths from eye for tying down material. Then cover the wire with wraps of thread.

Step 2. Tie in tail of yellow marabou a little longer than the shank of the hook. Secure with a half hitch.

Step 3. Tie in three pieces of yellow rubber equidistant from each other on top of the wraps of lead wire. Secure with a half hitch. Tie in the chenille.

Step 4. Wrap the chenille side by side to the eye and tie it down. Tie off and glue.

Girdle Bugger strikes at dusk.

Devil Leech

In July of 1973 I was selected to represent the United States at an exhibit held in Ufa, a small city in central Russia (then the Soviet Union) with a population of about 900,000 people. It had only been visited by Americans once back in the 1930s. My choice of destinations was between Moscow or Ufa, and I chose the latter as it sounded much more interesting in both the size and the possibilities to go fishing. I was glad of my choice, because I stayed in Moscow two weeks anyway and, more importantly, fished almost every day during the two months I was in Ufa.

What a great summer. The exhibit was called "Outdoor Recreation USA." It demonstrated to the Soviets what we Americans do on our leisure time—camping, fishing, hunting, sailing, skiing, boating, and all kinds of sports. My job was to demonstrate fly tying and fly casting, but I got some extra duty. The guy who was supposed to run the snow skiing booth got sick for a week. As I was a ski instructor back home, I also got to demo one of my other favorite sports.

Success with the Devil Leech.

What I didn't expect was the availability of so much fishing. There were three large rivers flowing through town and dozens of lakes and reservoirs nearby, so after work almost every night I could wet a line. At first, I caught very few fish, but with close examination, I observed that the stream bottoms were extremely dark, so I designed a streamer tied mostly of black leech yarn; it was an instant success. When I got back to the States, we refined the pattern by adding black Tasmanian devil hair, making it one of our deadliest streamers of all time. This incredible pattern has totally replaced the woolly bugger in my fly box mainly for three reasons: fantastic *natural* action in the water, great durability, and the fact that it doesn't *foul* like other subsurface flies.

DEVIL LEECH MATERIALS

Hook 3X long streamer hook

Thread 3/0

Weight lead wire .020

Tail Tasmanian devil hair and Krystal Flash

Body leech yarn

Wing Tasmanian devil hair and Krystal Flash

DEVIL LEECH TYING INSTRUCTIONS

Step 1. Lead hook with sixteen wraps of the lead wire, side by side. The Tasmanian devil hair has different lengths in it, so cut off a small bunch from the patch and pull out some of the shorter fibers to start the tail. Lay it on the shank just over the barb, wrap it in the middle, fold it back, and tie it down.

Step 2. Build tail. Then pull out some a little bit longer and tie it in the middle and fold it back and tie in some a little longer again, repeating this until you have the tail as long as you want it. Secure with a half hitch. Tying in the tail this way helps keep it from fouling. Tie in some Krystal Flash on the sides of the tail to give the fly some flash.

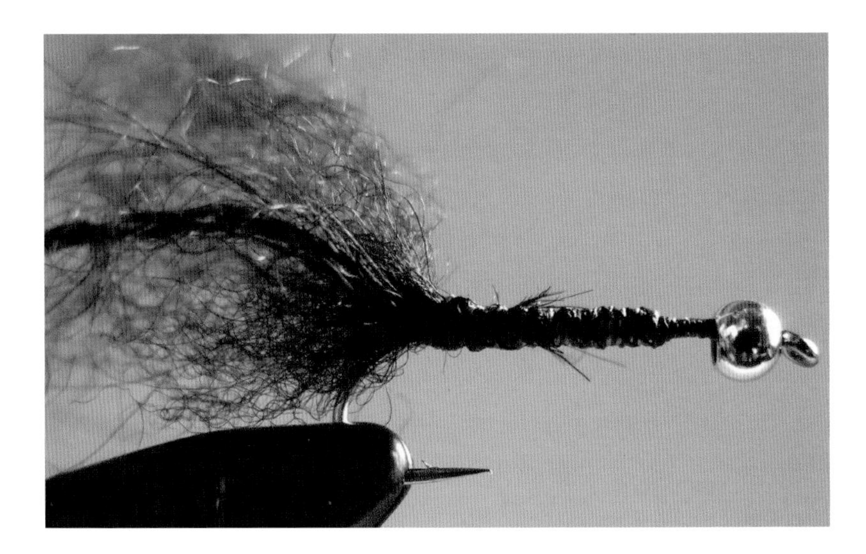

Step 3. Tie in some leech yarn. Secure with a half hitch.

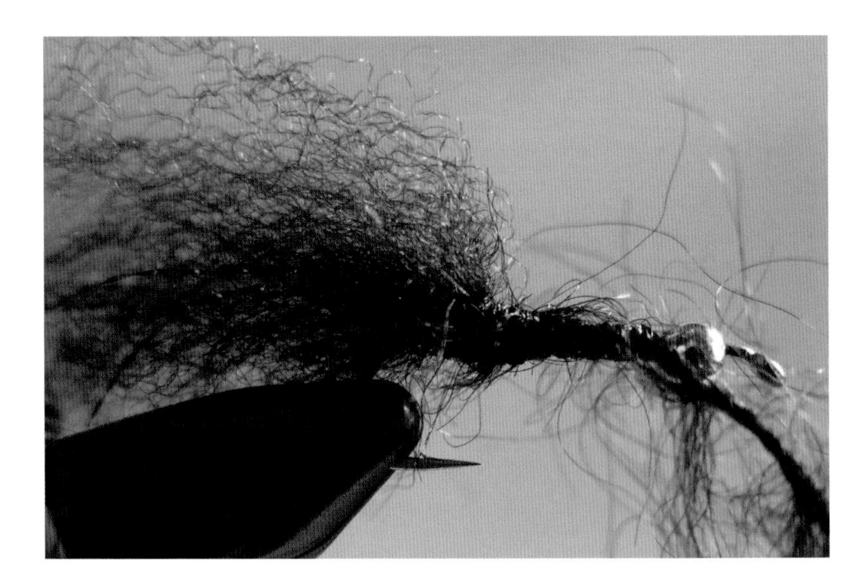

Step 4. Tie in the Tasmanian devil hair with the leech yarn rather than thread. Use medium-length Tasmanian devil hair for the wing. Lay a small amount of the Tasmanian devil hair on the shank and take one wrap of yarn around the Tasmanian devil hair and the shank. Then hold up the Tasmanian devil hair and make two tight wraps of yarn, holding the leech yarn securely in your hand.

Step 5. Proceed tying in the Tasmanian devil hair until you get to a point one and one-half eye-lengths before the eye. Then tie off the leech yarn and secure with a half hitch. Tie in some Krystal Flash on each side again to give the front of the fly some flash. Make another loop of Tasmanian devil hair and tying it in with the thread, tie it down securely. Tie off the fly, then brush the fly with a Velcro brush or piece of Velcro to make it look shaggy. (To make a Velcro brush, we glue a piece of Velcro on a tongue depressor.) To glue, put clear nail polish or head cement along where you tied in the wing with a tube applicator. This keeps the Tasmanian devil hair from pulling out where it is wrapped with the leech yarn.

Whopper on a Rub-A-Dub Streamer.

Rub-A-Dub Streamer

Ever since our introduction of the action dubbings back in 2000, our fishing seems to get better every year. This improvement parallels the fact that we keep finding more uses for the Wigglys, such as tails, legs, beards, collars, hackles, brushes, and other body parts. I really doubt we are better at casting and presentation than we were at a younger age. The use of more and more Wigglys in our modern-day Rub-A-Dub Streamers, simply put, gives our flies incredible action and results in many more strikes and higher rates of hookups. With the great new colors available, especially with the advent of glow-in-the-dark and ultraviolet, you can come up with some dynamite Rub-A-Dub patterns. The Rub-A-Dub Streamer has been very productive in rivers and lakes.

RUB-A-DUB STREAMER MATERIALS

Hook 3X long streamer hook

Thread 6/0

Bead gold

Tail gator hair and small amount of enhancer

Body dubbing brush made of Rub-A-Dub dubbing, gator hair, black enhancer, and Rub-A-Dub Wigglys (known as our streamer brush)

RUB-A-DUB STREAMER TYING INSTRUCTIONS

Step 1. Place gold bead on hook and tie on tail about one-quarter of an inch forward of the barb. The tail is made of gator hair with a little enhancer on the top of the gator hair. Tie down to just over barb. Secure with half hitch.

Step 2. Tie on the streamer brush just above the barb.

Step 3. Wrap it to the bead, brushing it back with your Velcro brush as you wrap, then tie down. (Make a Velcro brush by gluing the male side of a piece of Velcro on a tongue depressor.) Secure with half hitch. Tie on some Rub-A-Dub Wigglys around the bead, and use longer Wigglys and tie them in the center and fold back. You only need six or seven strands of Wigglys. It gives the fly more action at the head. Tie fly off and glue.

Fighting the big one.

All Black

During our last trip to New Zealand and Chile, we had some awesome experiences with the Velcro flies. On both streams and lakes, we caught many of our best fish on a relatively small, sparsely tied black Velcro streamer, no eyes, no crystal flash, and no bright colors blended in. It was developed while we were fishing in New Zealand, so we named it the All Black in honor of their great rugby team, which was world champion that year. I am sure the reason it is deadly is it imitates the black leeches found in most of the waters we fish. Since it was developed, it has worked extremely well all over the States and up in Canada on the Bow and Elk Rivers.

A little tip: if you go to New Zealand, first of all, take a handful of All Blacks (size 8) and, most importantly, fish them very carefully, on a floating line, at the tails of big pools, in shallow, slow-moving water, with long cross-current casts and continually mending downstream. This technique is deadly on rivers like the Mataura on the South Island as well as our rivers in the United States.

ALL BLACK MATERIALS

Hook stinger hook size 8

Weight lead wire .035

Head medium black Velcro dot (male side)

Wing black fish fuzz

ALL BLACK TYING INSTRUCTIONS

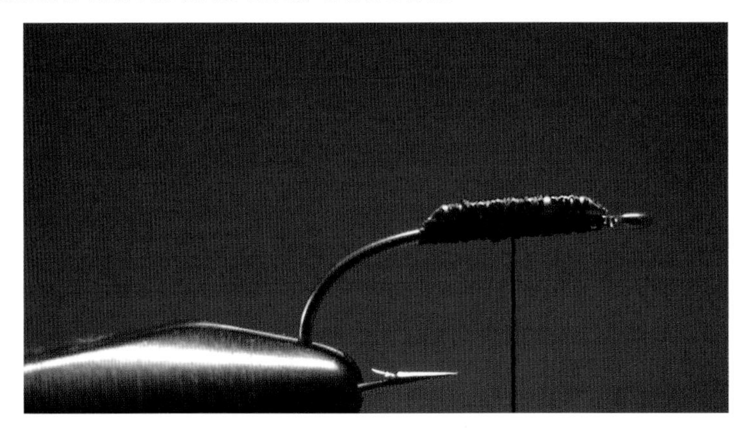

Step 1. Cut a little more than a quarter of an inch of lead wire and tie on top of shank firmly at a point one eye-length from eye. Superglue it and let dry. This will keep the Velcro dot from slipping to the side.

Step 2. Tie in the wing. We tie in a fairly short, sparse wing, only about an inch and a quarter long. We usually tie in two clumps, the first a little shorter than the second.

Step 3. Take a medium black Velcro dot, fold to trim. Leave the plastic on the back.

Step 4. Trim the Velcro to shape of fish head when folded.

Step 5. Cover the sides and top of the area where the lead and wing are tied in with superglue; this glues the Velcro to the fly. Remove the plastic from the back of the Velcro, then bring the trimmed Velcro from underneath up over the body of the fly with the larger part of the Velcro just behind the eye and press together firmly. Glue the edges of the Velcro.

MANTILLA

Some marine biologists claim that a newborn minnow, for the first few minutes after it hatches from the egg, has a thin membrane over the eyes, making it very vulnerable prey to bigger fish. We do not know if this is true, but if the success of both of our new patterns, the Mantilla and Veil Fly, is any indication, it is probably correct. The eyes are masked until they get completely wet and then they become quite visible. This was one of our deadliest imitations last year in smaller streams and lakes. It usually fished best near the surface, using a dressed leader, or slightly under, with no floatant on the leader. A very slow retrieve with no twitch was also very effective.

MANTILLA MATERIALS

Hook stinger hook

Thread 6/0

Tail synthetic living fibers (mixed colors)

Body white #1 glow-in-the-dark chenille

Eye red awesome eyes (stick-on 3 mil)

Veil synthetic living fibers (mixed colors)

MANTILLA TYING INSTRUCTIONS

Step 1. Tie on tail at a point about one-quarter inch forward of barb, then tie on glow-in-the-dark chenille. Secure with half hitch.

Step 2. Wrap the chenille over itself to make a thicker body. Secure with half hitch. Glue on the stick-on eyes with superglue at a point about the length of the eye from where you tied down the chenille. Let dry.

Step 3. Tie on synthetic living fibers in thin clumps between the glow-in-the-dark chenille and the eye of the hook, then fold back and tie it down. Repeat this three or four times. This makes the veil on the fly. Make sure the fly is covered all the way around between the glow-in-the-dark chenille and the eye of the hook.

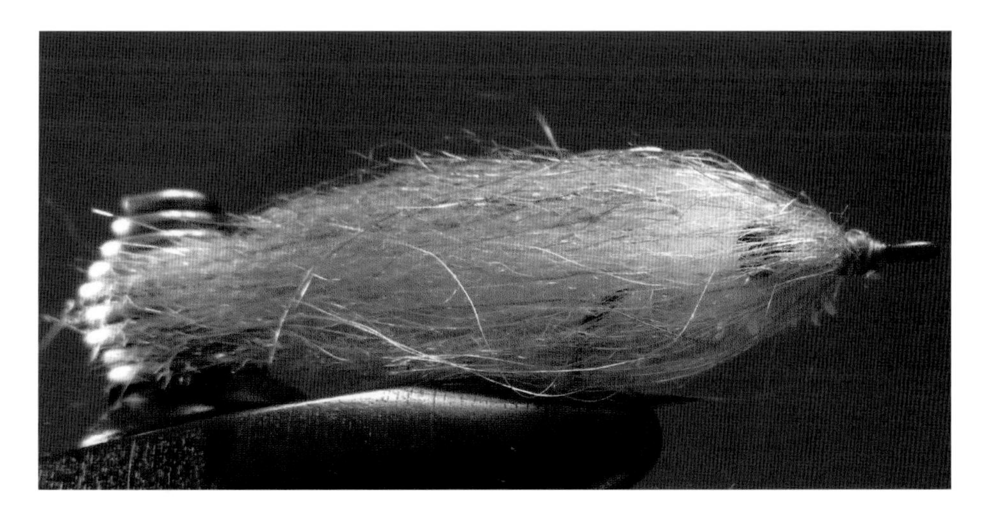

Step 4. Tie down the synthetic living fibers well and glue. Trim any synthetic living fibers that are too long.

The beauty of fall fishing.

Veil Fly

The success of the Mantilla was so exciting we decided to add another version of the newborn minnow to our repertoire. Actually, the introduction of two new tying materials influenced our decision as much as anything: crystal web synthetic fibers and a super bright glow-in-the-dark material. Crystal web made fantastic brushes; it is perfect for constructing the membrane that covers the eyes, which were easily stamped out of the new glow-in-the-dark tape.

The Veil was deadly the very first day we fished it. My favorite method of presenting the fly was to make a relatively long cast in a knee-deep riffle, using a floating fly line, with a stop-and-go, fairly fast retrieve. Probably the most productive technique would be to use a full sinker or a fast-sink tip and strip very quickly. Here is a little suggestion: a big part of streamer fishing is coverage, so the faster you strip, the more water you cover in a day of fishing. Also, I find the more aggressive I fish, the more aggressively fish attack the fly. Especially in new water, I try to cover it all. We use a purple color for this fly quite often for Georgetown Lake, as it is a great color to fish there. You can use the color of your choice.

VEIL FLY MATERIALS

Hook stinger hook 3366

Thread fluorescent chartreuse ultra thread

Tail clear crystal web and light lavender crystal web

Body purple chenille (or color of your choice)

Eyes glow-in-the-dark tape (eyes punched out with a paper punch)

Veil dubbing brush made of light lavender crystal web

VEIL FLY TYING INSTRUCTIONS

Step 1. Tie on a small clump of clear crystal web at a point about halfway on the shank. Then on top of that, tie on a small clump of light lavender crystal web. Wrap thread back to the barb, length depending on the size of fly you are tying, usually about one and one-half times the length of the body. Secure with a half hitch. Tie on purple chenille at the point above the barb.

Step 2. Wrap the purple chenille to about two eye-lengths from the eye. Double wrap the chenille, making the body thicker so the eye will show up well. Punch the eye out of the glow-in-the-dark tape with a paper punch. Put a little drop of superglue on the chenille where you are going to place the eye. Place eye, let dry, then put glue over the eye. Repeat on other side.

Step 3. Tie on the crystal web dubbing brush and make about three or four wraps, leaving plenty of room for your smooth tie off. Glue tie off.

Man, what a brown!

Little Ripper

This gorgeous fly is one of our new creations that we are sure would work for anything that swims. It is another brainchild we undoubtedly created because of two exciting fly-tying materials recently put on the market by our good friend, the "Mad Scientist." The first material is a very shiny metallic, light-reflecting product called Northern Lights that will dress up any pattern. For the Little Ripper, we use it as the tail with a beautiful blend of an olive-yellow color. This material comes in thirty colors with more on the way. The other material, used for the wing, is one of our favorite action dubbings called Kraken with lots of long and short Wigglys. It is so easy to tie with and creates awesome streamers that are not only deadly, but easy to cast. Last year, fishing with this fly was unbelievable; the fish seem to be really turned on by the pattern and the colors as it worked well everywhere we fished it.

Nice one on the Little Ripper.

LITTLE RIPPER MATERIALS

Hook stinger hook-3366

Eyes hourglass eyes (micro)

Thread fluorescent chartreuse ultra thread

Tail Northern Lights (olive-yellow)

Wing Kraken dubbing (perch color)

LITTLE RIPPER TYING INSTRUCTIONS

Step 1. Tie on eyes on the underside of the hook a little over one eye-length from eye. Tie on the tail of Northern Lights right behind the eyes and wrap with thread to just above barb.

Step 2. Tie on the Kraken dubbing in small bunches, first just in front of the middle of the shank. Lay a small bunch on top of the hook, make a wrap with the thread in the middle of the bunch, then fold the Kraken back over itself and secure.

Step 3. Then tie small bunches on each side the same way. Then one more small bunch in the middle over the eyes.

Step 4. Tie on four or five strands of Northern Lights between the eyes and the eye of the hook, leaving the ends sticking up over the wing. Wrap the Northern Lights around the eyes, covering top and bottom, then secure and tie off. Glue the Northern Lights around the head with superglue so it will not be torn off.

Eradicator

In 2015 when we started tying and testing our new UV-X materials, one of the streamers we made was of a beautiful synthetic dubbing called Kraken with long and short black Wigglys and some ultraviolet enhancer. The abdomen is made of an ultraviolet dubbing that has no Wigglys but glows beautifully. We went to Georgetown Lake, about three hours from our home, and fished some of our other flies. Then I decided to put this new black ultraviolet streamer on to test. Wow, the fish were all over it. Big ones as well as smaller ones. After that we fished it everywhere we went, rivers and lakes, and the pattern worked well. It has a black bead, but if we want to go deeper, we just use a sink-tip line. We decided this would be our first ultraviolet streamer. We named it the Eradicator.

ERADICATOR MATERIALS

Hook 3X long size 10

Thread fluorescent chartreuse ultra thread

Bead black brass

Tail black UV-X Kraken dubbing

Abdomen light olive UV-X nymph dubbing

Wing black UV-X Kraken dubbing

ERADICATOR TYING INSTRUCTIONS

Step 1. Put bead on hook, then wrap thread on hook to form a good base. Tie on tail of black Kraken dubbing from a point about in the middle of the shank to a point above the barb. Secure with a half hitch.

Step 2. Dub over tail tie in with the nymph dubbing. You may want to use some dubbing wax on your thread. Tie in a small clump of Kraken dubbing by laying the Kraken on top of the shank, tying down in the middle, and folding the forward part back over the back part, and tying it down just at the fold, forming a small wing. Secure with a half hitch. Dub over that tie in.

Step 3. Tie in another clump of Kraken the same way: tie down in the middle and fold back, on the top of the shank of the hook. Secure with a half hitch. Then tie in two more small clumps the same way, one on each side of the shank, and tie down; then tie one more small clump and fold back, right behind the bead. Tie off. Brush with your Velcro brush and glue.

Step 4. Eradicator glowing under UV light.

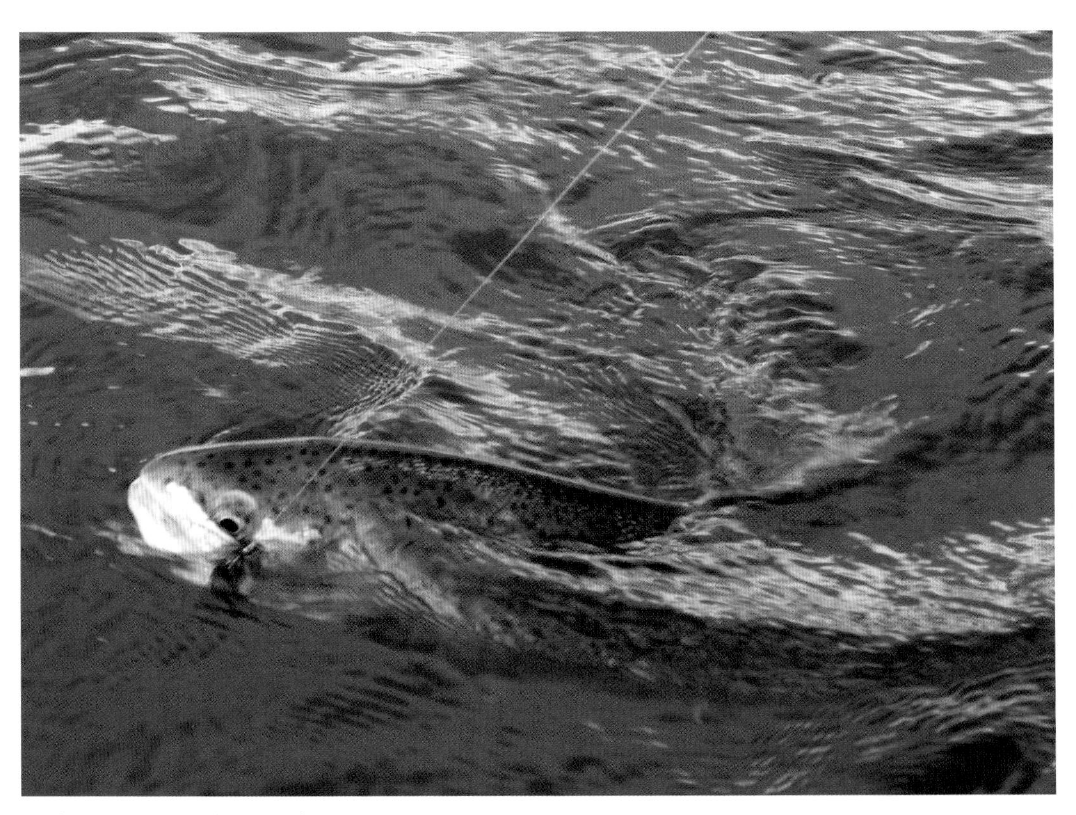

Fish caught on the Eradicator.

Glitzy Legs

This pattern, much like our Georgie Long Legs and Peacock Long Legs, has an incredible action in the water. Not only do the legs generate a crazy swimming movement, but they are made from a great glow-in-the-dark synthetic fiber, similar to a five-weight fly line. As mentioned earlier, I carry a small, portable camera flash to keep the legs charged up, although, if it is a bright sunny day, that's all you need for about ten minutes. In testing these flies we found the fish take them just under the surface or deeper, and when you are fishing them just under the surface, you see the strike just like a dry fly. There is a large pond we go to that is quite deep. We use a sinking line, flash the fly, and let the fly sink, then start stripping it at a medium speed. This technique has been very effective. It does not have to be dark to fish the glow-in-the-dark flies.

GLITZY LEGS MATERIALS

Hook stinger hook 3366

Thread fluorescent chartreuse ultra thread #140

Eyes black bead chain

Tail orange glow-in-the-dark Flashabou

Legs aqua glow ribbing

Body glow-in-the-dark super floss

Thorax glow-in-the-dark dubbing brush (mixed colors)

GLITZY LEGS TYING INSTRUCTIONS

Step 1. Tie the bead chain eyes on the underside of the hook about one and one-half eye-lengths in back of the eye. Secure with half hitch. Tie on tail of glow-in-the-dark Flashabou, starting at the halfway point on the hook and wrap to just above the barb. Secure with half hitch. Tie on the glow-in-the-dark super floss at that point. Secure with half hitch.

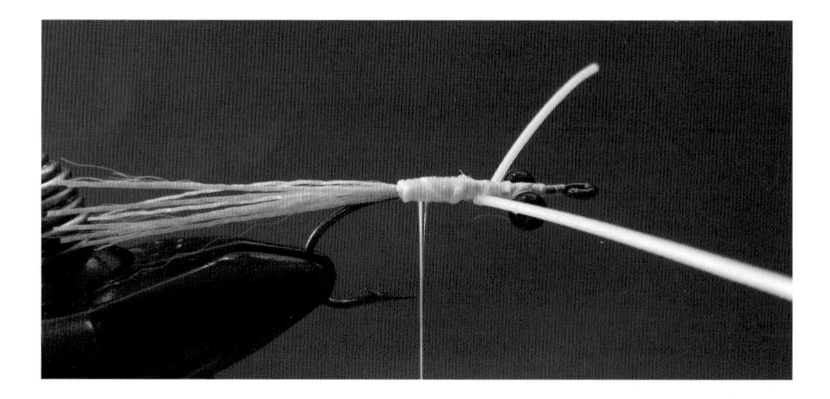

Step 2. Wrap the glow-in-the-dark super floss, covering the tail tie in. Secure with half hitch. Tie in legs on the underside of the hook. Tie the legs on in the middle of the piece of aqua glow ribbing. The legs are precut aqua glow legs. As you tie them to the shank of the hook, bend them forward. Secure with half hitch.

Step 3. Tie on the glow-in-the-dark dubbing brush at the point where you quit wrapping the super floss. Wrap it forward around the eyes and tie it down. Tie off the fly and glue.

Step 4. Trim the brush to make all the fibers about the same length. Side view of fly glowing.

Alternate view. Fly glowing from the top.

AFTERWORD

This book has covered some of the highlights of things we've done in the world of fly tying and fly fishing over the past few years. Before this period, we physically travelled around to some of the great fishing places, including New Zealand, Alaska, Chile, and all over the United States, to test our patterns and techniques. Now that we've decided to settle down in Western Montana, we feel we've found the best place of all. Where else can you find an area with so many great bodies of water, streams, rivers, and hungry trout?

So, over the next few years, I'm sure we will develop many more patterns. Just remember, someone can give the right fly, but, no one can cast for you!

Best wishes for rising trout and matched hatches!

Index